DISCOVERING THE UNITED STATES

Florida

BY ANGELA LIM

Kids Core
An Imprint of Abdo Publishing
abdobooks.com

abdobooks.com

Printed in China.
052024
092024

THIS BOOK CONTAINS RECYCLED MATERIALS

Cover Photo: Michael Orso/Moment/Getty Images
Interior Photos: Jacqueline Nell/Disneyland Resort/Getty Images Entertainment/Getty Images, 4–5; Steve Byland/Shutterstock Images, 7 (top left); iStockphoto, 7 (top right), 8, 14, 26, 28 (bottom); Shutterstock Images, 7 (bottom left), 20–21, 24; Rejean Bedard/iStockphoto, 7 (bottom right); Felix Mizioznikov/Shutterstock Images, 10; Zak Bennett/AFP/Getty Images, 12–13; Jeff Greenberg/Universal Images Group/Getty Images, 17; Songquan Deng/Shutterstock Images, 18, 28 (top left); Danita Delimont/Shutterstock Images, 23; Red Line Editorial, 28 (top right), 29

Editor: Laura Stickney
Series Designer: Katharine Hale

Library of Congress Control Number: 2023949333

Publisher's Cataloging-in-Publication Data

Names: Lim, Angela, author.
Title: Florida / by Angela Lim
Description: Minneapolis, Minnesota: Abdo Publishing, 2025 | Series: Discovering the United States | Includes online resources and index.
Identifiers: ISBN 9781098293796 (lib. bdg.) | ISBN 9798384913061 (ebook)
Subjects: LCSH: U.S. states--Juvenile literature. | Florida--History--Juvenile literature. | Southeastern States--Juvenile literature. | Physical geography--United States--Juvenile literature.
Classification: DDC 973--dc23

All population data taken from:
"Estimates of Population by Sex, Race, and Hispanic Origin: April 1, 2020 to July 1, 2022." *US Census Bureau, Population Division*, June 2023, census.gov.

CONTENTS

CHAPTER 1
A Grand Opening 4

CHAPTER 2
The People of Florida 12

CHAPTER 3
Places in Florida 20

State Map 28
Glossary 30
Online Resources 31
Learn More 31
Index 32
About the Author 32

Disney World hosts several special celebration events each year.

CHAPTER 1

A Grand Opening

October 1, 1971, was a warm day in Orlando, Florida. But something new was happening in the city. That day, the gates to Walt Disney World opened for the first time. More than 10,000 visitors went to the brand-new theme park on its opening day.

There was a celebratory parade. More than 1,000 marching band members from across Florida performed. People released hundreds of balloons into the sky.

A person in a Mickey Mouse costume greeted park visitors. The towers of Cinderella's Castle seemed to touch the clouds. Families enjoyed the park's many rides, such as It's a Small World. This musical boat ride takes visitors along a waterway. Childlike puppets sing and dance.

Disney World continues to attract tourists. The park has added new rides since its opening. Disney World has two waterparks and four theme parks, including the Magic Kingdom. In 2022, about 57,000 people visited the Magic Kingdom each day.

Florida Facts

DATE OF STATEHOOD
March 3, 1845

CAPITAL
Tallahassee

POPULATION
22,244,823

AREA
65,758 square miles (170,312 sq km)

STATE BIRD

Mockingbird

STATE TREE

Sabal palm

STATE FLOWER

Orange blossom

STATE ANIMAL

Panther

Each US state has a different population, size, and capital city. States also have state symbols.

Florida's Land

Florida is part of the US region called the South. Alabama and Georgia border the state to the north. Florida also borders two bodies of water.

South Beach in Miami is on the Atlantic Ocean. It is one of the most popular beaches in the United States.

The Atlantic Ocean lies to the east. To the south and west is the Gulf of Mexico.

Florida is the flattest state in the country. Most of the state lies close to sea level. However, Florida features many different landscapes.

It has forests and **prairies**. The Everglades are an important wetland region in the state. Many animals live there, including panthers and manatees. There are **coral reefs** offshore. Florida also has more than 4,500 islands. The Florida Keys are a group of islands off the state's southern coast.

Florida's Shores

Florida has the longest shoreline in the **continental** United States. It streches for 8,436 miles (13,576 km). That distance includes the state's many islands.

In 2022, Hurricane Ian caused $112 billion in damage throughout Florida.

Florida's Climate

Florida is nicknamed the Sunshine State. It is known for its sunny weather. People living in Florida see about 230 days of sunshine each year. But the state also gets a lot of rain. Hurricanes and tropical storms can affect Florida.

Summers in Florida are hot and **humid**. Winters are mild. The warm weather attracts many visitors to the state. Some people who live in colder northern states and Canada choose to spend most winter months in Florida.

Explore Online

Visit the website below. Does it give any new information about Florida that wasn't in Chapter One?

Further Evidence

abdocorelibrary.com/discovering-florida

Daniel Tommie, a member of the Seminole nation, carves a traditional canoe. In 2019, Florida's Seminole nation had roughly 3,000 members.

CHAPTER 2

The People of Florida

The first people arrived in Florida about 12,000 years ago. They formed American Indian nations such as the Timucua, Calusa, and Apalachee. By the 1500s, around 100,000 American Indians lived in the area.

This version of the Florida state flag was first used in 1900. It has been updated many times, most recently in 1985.

In 1513, Spanish explorer Juan Ponce de León arrived. He named the land Florida. This name comes from a Spanish celebration called *Pascua Florida*, or "feast of the flowers."

Many Spanish and French people moved into Florida during the 1500s. They brought diseases that killed thousands of American Indians.

The United Kingdom took over control of Florida in 1763. Many American Indians died during this period as well due to new diseases. Others moved to Alabama and Louisiana.

Slavery in Florida

Spanish explorers brought the first enslaved Black people to Florida in 1526. Slavery remained legal when Florida became a state in 1845. At the time, many Black people in Florida were enslaved. Slavery was legal nationwide until 1865.

Today, two federally recognized American Indian nations live in Florida. They are the Seminole and Miccosukee. Some of their members live on **reservations**.

Today, about 77 percent of Floridians are white. Twenty-seven percent are Hispanic or Latino, and 17 percent are Black. Less than 1 percent are American Indian.

Culture

Florida is influenced by Cuban culture. In the 1960s, thousands of Cuban **refugees** moved to Florida. Many Cuban families live in Little Havana. This neighborhood is in the city of Miami. Visitors can go salsa dancing. They can enjoy Cuban foods, such as Cuban sandwiches.

Little Havana's *Calle Ocho*, or "Eighth Street," is famous for its food scene.

Café con leche is a popular drink. It is espresso made with Cuban coffee.

Florida has Greek influences too. In the 1900s, many Greek people moved to Tarpon Springs. This city has Greek bakeries and shops.

Industries

The space industry is important in Florida. In 1958, the US government created the National **Aeronautics** and Space Administration (NASA).

Visitors to the Kennedy Space Center can stroll through the Rocket Garden, which is filled with real rockets once used by NASA.

In 1962, NASA opened the Kennedy Space Center in Florida. The Apollo 11 mission launched from this site in 1969. Astronauts on this mission became the first people to walk on the moon. Eastern Florida is often called the Space Coast.

Tourism and farming are other major industries in Florida. More than 137 million tourists visited the state in 2022. Florida farmers produce crops such as sugarcane and citrus fruits.

Primary Source

Jeanette Nuñez is a Florida politician. She talked about the state's space industry in 2023:

> It may have started on the Space Coast, but now all of Florida is . . . breaking boundaries to claim many firsts in aerospace. . . . If you want to soar among the stars, your journey begins in Florida.

Source: Jeanette Nuñez. "Florida's Space Economy: The Future Is Now." *Space News*, 7 Mar. 2023, spacenews.com. Accessed 5 Oct. 2023.

What's the Big Idea?

What is this quote's main idea? Explain how the main idea is supported by details.

Jacksonville covers 747 square miles (1,935 sq km).

CHAPTER 3

Places in Florida

The capital of Florida is Tallahassee. But Jacksonville is the state's largest city. More than 970,000 people call Jacksonville home. This city is located in northeastern Florida. It is also the largest city by land area in the continental United States.

Jacksonville is home to the Jacksonville Jaguars, a National Football League (NFL) team.

Other major cities in Florida include Miami and Tampa. Miami is on the state's southeastern coast. It has many white, sandy beaches. The city also has museums and gardens. Tampa is a coastal city in western Florida. It is home to the Florida Aquarium. Busch Gardens is a popular amusement park in the city.

Florida Sports

Many top-level sports teams play in Florida. The state has three teams in the NFL. Florida's Major League Baseball teams are based in Miami and Tampa. The state also has two major professional hockey teams and two basketball teams.

Crocodiles can be seen in the Everglades. Florida is the only US state in which crocodiles live.

Parks and Landmarks

Florida has several national parks. Everglades National Park attracts more than 1 million visitors each year. The park is on the southern tip of Florida. It protects wetlands that are home to many types of plants and animals.

Construction began on Fort Jefferson in 1846. The fort was never finished.

People visit the park to see alligators, crocodiles, and more than 360 types of birds.

Biscayne National Park is off the southeastern coast of Florida. Visitors can snorkel and see shipwrecks underwater. Dry Tortugas National Park is 70 miles (113 km) west of Key West. The park protects coral reefs. It also has a historic US military fort called Fort Jefferson.

Landmarks

Famous landmarks also bring visitors to Florida. More than 58 million people go to Disney World each year. The theme park has rides and other entertainment for people of all ages.

At the Kennedy Space Center, people can learn about space history. They can also learn about the future of space travel. The center features exhibits that show NASA's plans to explore Mars and other parts of space.

Key West is the southernmost city in the continental United States.

The southernmost point of the continental United States is located on Key West. People can take pictures next to a giant **buoy** that marks the spot. The Castillo de San Marcos is another important landmark. It is a Spanish fort in the city of Saint Augustine in northeast Florida.

Florida has beautiful beaches and natural wonders. People looking for a thrill may visit the state's theme parks. Or they can try delicious Cuban and Greek foods. The state has many places and activities that everyone can enjoy.

Further Evidence

Look at the website below. Does it give any new evidence to support Chapter Three?

Where Are the Everglades?

abdocorelibrary.com/discovering-florida

State Map

KEY

Capital
Park
City or town
Point of interest

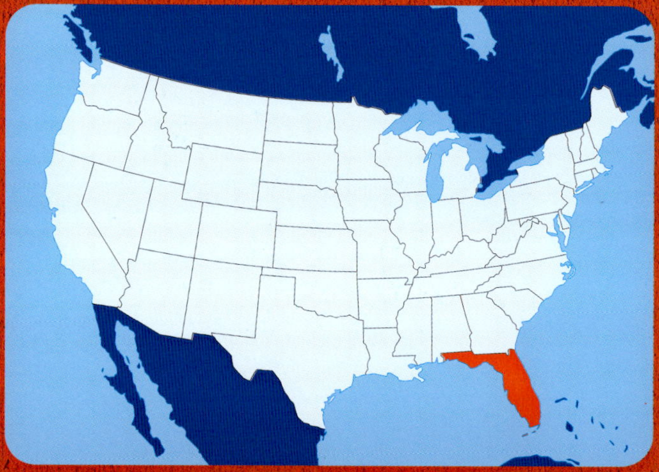

Kennedy Space Center

Miami

Florida: The Sunshine State

Glossary

aeronautics
the science of flight, aircraft, and spacecraft

buoy
a floating object that marks an underwater location

continental
connected on a body of land

coral reefs
underwater habitats formed by living things called coral

humid
describing air that has a lot of moisture

prairies
areas of flat grasslands

refugees
people who leave a country to escape danger

reservations
lands set aside by a government for a specific group of people

Online Resources

To learn more about Florida, visit our free resource websites below.

Core Library CONNECTION
FREE! COMMON CORE MULTIMEDIA RESOURCES

Visit **abdocorelibrary.com** or scan this QR code for free Common Core resources for teachers and students, including vetted activities, multimedia, and booklinks, for deeper subject comprehension.

Booklinks NONFICTION NETWORK
FREE! ONLINE NONFICTION RESOURCES

Visit **abdobooklinks.com** or scan this QR code for free additional online weblinks for further learning. These links are routinely monitored and updated to provide the most current information available.

Learn More

Abdo, Kenny. *Jacksonville Jaguars.* Abdo, 2022.

Payne, Stefanie. *The National Parks.* DK, 2020.

Tieck, Sarah. *Florida.* Abdo, 2020.

Index

Apalachee nation, 13

Calusa nation, 13

Disney World, 5–6, 25

Everglades, 9, 23

food, 16–17, 27

Jacksonville, 21–22

Key West, 25–26

Miami, 16, 22
Miccosukee nation, 16

National Aeronautics and Space Administration (NASA), 17–18, 25

Orlando, 5

parks, 23–25
Ponce de León, Juan, 14

Saint Augustine, 27
Seminole nation, 16
sports, 22

Tampa, 22
Timucua nation, 13

About the Author

Angela Lim is an MFA student in poetry at Indiana University in Bloomington, Indiana.